WORLD'S LONGEST-LIVING ANIMALS
250-YEAR-OLD
TUBE WORMS!
I0817374
By Joni Kelly
Gareth Stevens
PUBLISHING

Please visit our website, www.garethstevens.com. For a free color catalog of all our high-quality books, call toll free 1-800-542-2595 or fax 1-877-542-2596.

Library of Congress Cataloging-in-Publication Data

Names: Kelly, Joni, author.
Title: 250-year-old tube worms! / Joni Kelly.
Other titles: Two hundred fifty year old tube worms
Description: New York : Gareth Stevens Publishing, [2019] | Series: World's longest-living animals | Includes index.
Identifiers: LCCN 2017029737| ISBN 9781538216903 (pbk.) | ISBN 9781538216910 (6 pack) | ISBN 9781538216897 (library bound)
Subjects: LCSH: Tube worms–Juvenile literature.
Classification: LCC QL391.A6 K45 2018 | DDC 592/.64–dc23
LC record available at https://lccn.loc.gov/2017029737https://lccn.loc.gov/2017029008

Published in 2019 by
Gareth Stevens Publishing
111 East 14th Street, Suite 349
New York, NY 10003

Designer: Andrea Davison-Bartolotta and Laura Bowen
Editor: Joan Stoltman

Photo credits: Cover, p. 1 Courtesy of NOAA Ocean Explorer/Lophelia II 2010: Oil Seeps and Deep Reefs; pp. 2–24 (background) Dmitrieva Olga/Shutterstock.com; pp. 5, 7, 13 Courtesy of NOAA; p. 11 Courtesy of NOAA/Okeanos Explorer Program, Galapagos Rift Expedition 2011; pp. 15, 19 Courtesy of NOAA/Gulf of Mexico Expedition 2002; p. 21 James Jones Jr/Shutterstock.com.

Printed in the United States of America

CPSIA compliance information: Batch #CS18GS: For further information contact Gareth Stevens, New York, New York at 1-800-542-2595.

CONTENTS

A Strange Discovery. 4

What's a Tube Worm? 6

Too Darn Hot 10

Can You Believe It?. 12

How Do They Do It?. 14

Very Important!. 18

Glossary. 22

For More Information. 23

Index 24

Boldface words appear in the glossary.

A Strange Discovery

We used to think the deep ocean was too cold, too dark, and too toxic for life. Then, in 1977, **scientists** discovered strange, giant animals living there! Tests showed that they were tube worms—but not like the tiny ones scientists had seen before.

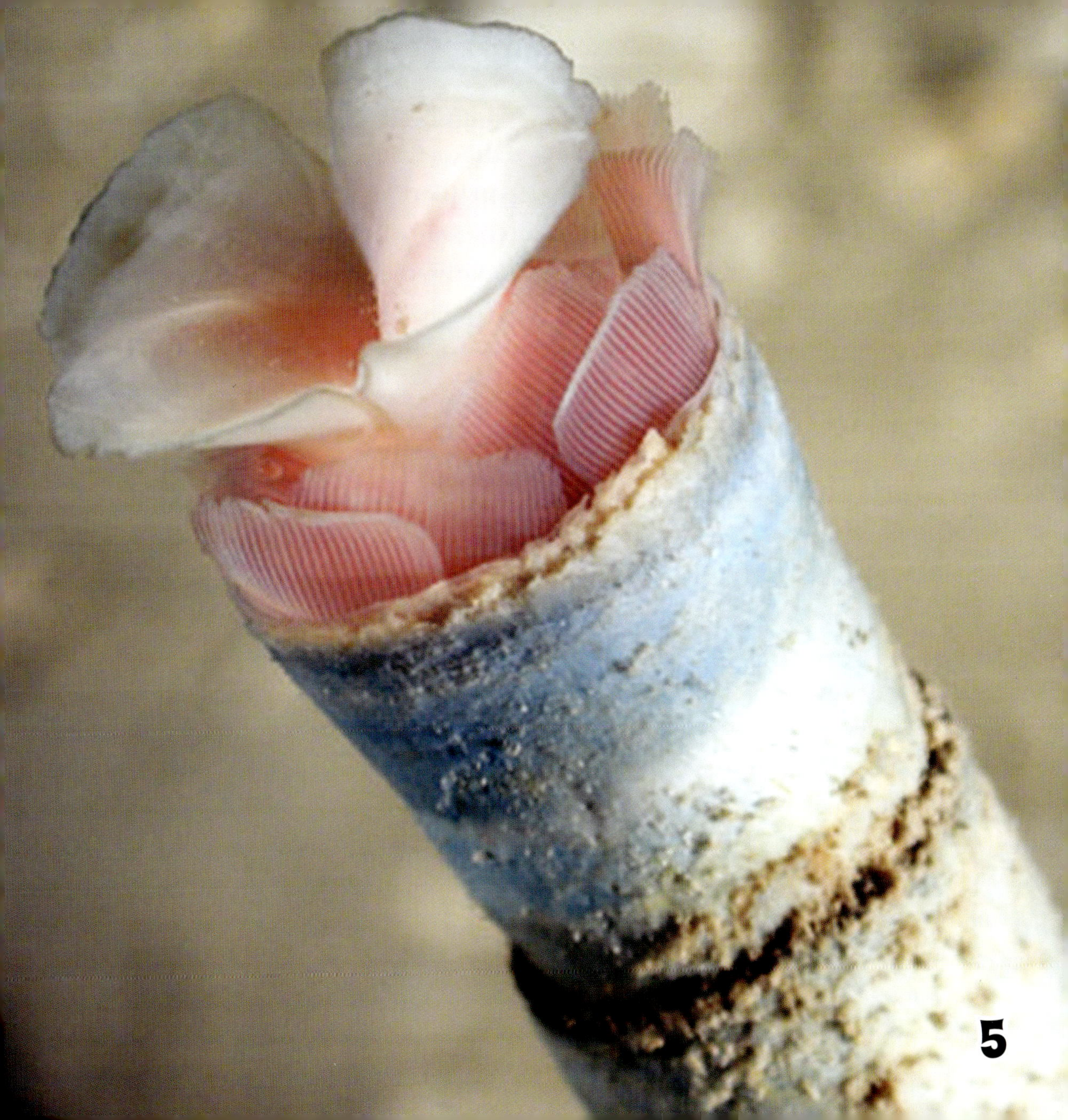

What's a Tube Worm?

Even though they have no eyes, legs, or mouth, tube worms are animals! They live inside a long, thin, **hollow** shell that can bend. It's made of the same matter as a crab or lobster shell. They live on rocks and don't move once they're adults.

Inside each tube worm are **billions** of bacteria. These bacteria change toxic matter into energy, which the tube worm uses to make food. Neither the worm nor the bacteria can **survive** without the other. This way of feeding is one of the biggest discoveries in a hundred years!

THE PARTS OF A TUBE WORM BODY

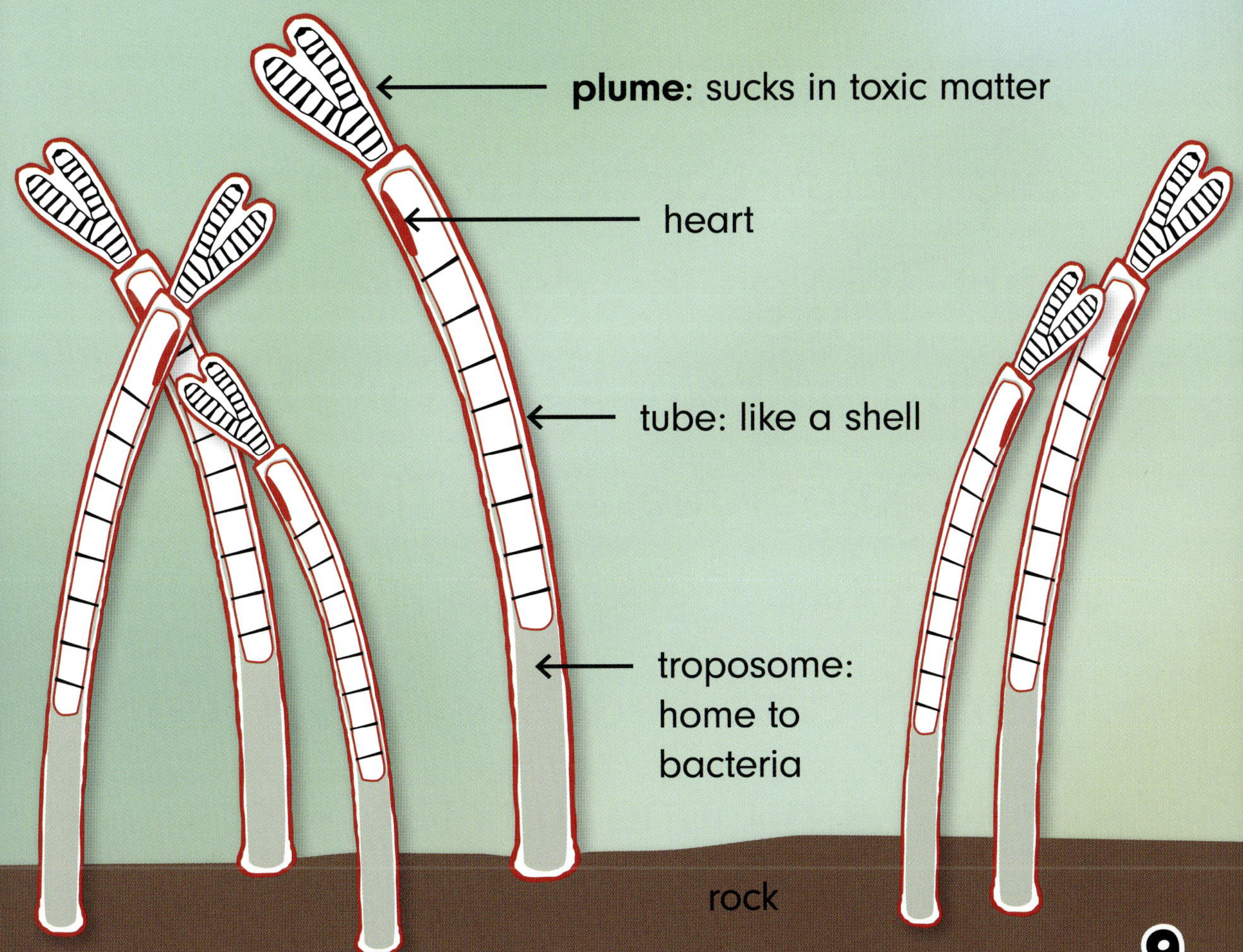

Too Darn Hot

The tube worms discovered in 1977 were living near **hydrothermal vents**. Though the deep sea is usually very cold, it's about 750°F (400°C) near the vents! These tube worms grew faster than all other **invertebrates**—reaching 6 to 8 feet (1.8 to 2.4 m) long in a few years.

Can You Believe It?

Even though the 1977 discovery of vent life was important, giant tube worms found in 1984 would prove to be an even bigger discovery. On **cold seeps** in the Gulf of Mexico, there were special, giant tube worms that could live 250 years—and maybe as long as 600 years!

How Do They Do It?

Tube worms that live near cold seeps are different from other tube worms. They can grow over 10 feet (3 m) tall. They grow from both ends. Their communities—called "bushes"—have "roots" just like a plant! They take up toxic matter through their roots to feed their bacteria.

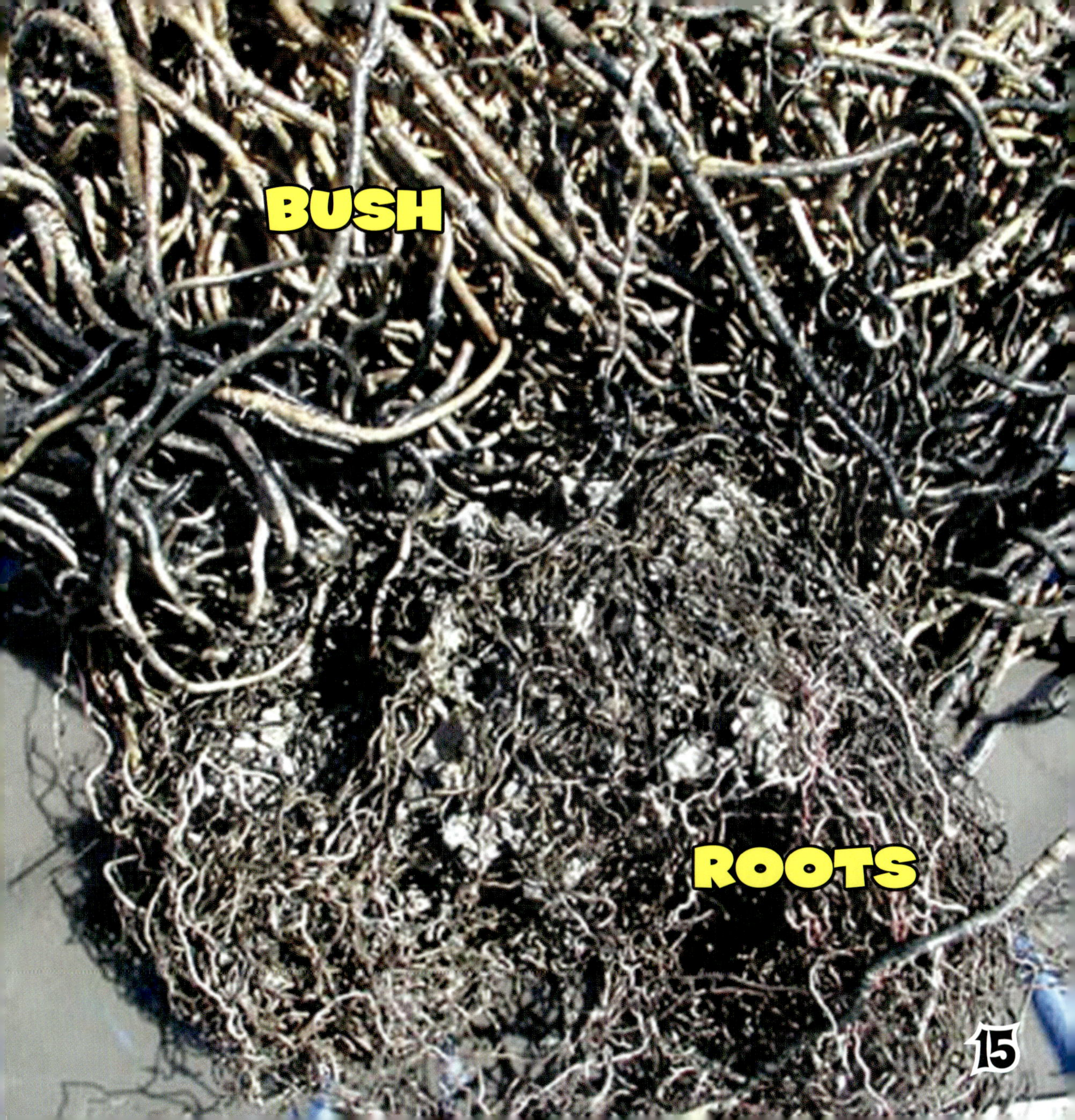
BUSH
ROOTS

Cold-seep tube worms put their waste into the ground through their roots. Then bacteria in the ground turn it back into food for the bacteria inside tube worms. Without this special way of recycling, these tube worms could only live about 40 years!

COLD-SEEP TUBE WORMS

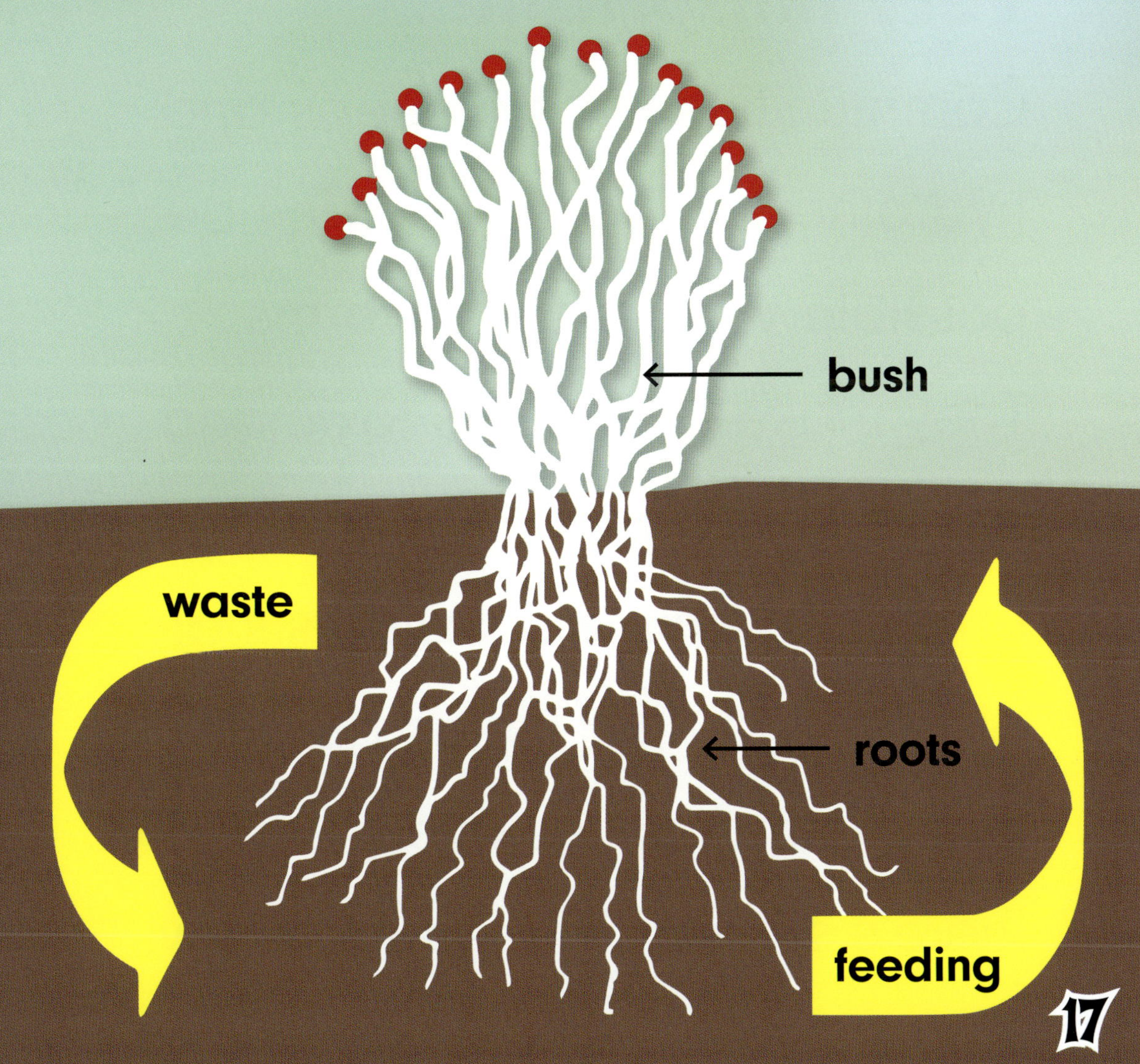

Very Important!

Communities in cold seeps and hydrothermal vents wouldn't be possible without tube worms. They make areas less toxic and give a safe home to hundreds of special animals. Scientists are discovering new things about these communities every year, but there's still much we don't know!

MUSSELS

Cold seeps let out the same high-value oil and gas that heats homes and powers cars. People want to drill to get to it, which hurts these communities. Then we'd never know how or why tube worms live so long!

DRILLING FOR OIL

GLOSSARY

billion: 1,000,000,000 or a thousand millions

cold seep: a place were oil and gases leak onto the ocean floor because of movement in the earth below

hollow: having nothing inside, not solid

hydrothermal vent: a place where water that's been heated underground comes out of the ground

invertebrate: a type of animal that does not have a backbone

plume: a part that spreads out into a shape like a feather

scientist: someone who studies the way things work and the way things are

survive: to live through something

FOR MORE INFORMATION

BOOKS

Davies, Nicola. *Monsters of the Deep*. Washington, DC: National Geographic Society, 2011.

Day, Nancy Raines. *Way Down Below Deep*. Gretna, LA: Pelican Publishing Company, 2014.

Moore, Heidi. *Giant Tube Worms and Other Interesting Invertebrates*. Chicago, IL: Raintree, 2012.

WEBSITES

Giant Tubeworms
amnh.org/explore/ology/ology-cards/186-giant-tubeworms
Read all about tube worms on the site for the American Natural History Museum.

Giant Tube Worms of the Galapagos
nautiluslive.org/video/2015/06/19/giant-tube-worms-galapagos
Watch this amazing video of tube worms deep under the sea.

Tube Worm
britannica.com/animal/tube-worm/images-videos
Check out videos and pictures of tube worms deep underwater.

Publisher's note to educators and parents: Our editors have carefully reviewed these websites to ensure that they are suitable for students. Many websites change frequently, however, and we cannot guarantee that a site's future contents will continue to meet our high standards of quality and educational value. Be advised that students should be closely supervised whenever they access the Internet.

INDEX

bacteria 8, 9, 14, 16

cold seeps 12, 14, 16, 17, 18, 20

communities 14, 15, 17, 18, 20

deep ocean 4, 10

food 8, 16

Gulf of Mexico 12

hydrothermal vents 10, 18

life-span 12, 16

roots 14, 16

scientists 4, 18

shell 6

size 10, 14

toxic 4, 8, 14, 18